CONTRACTS LAW LECTURE NOTES

CONTENTS OUTLINE

CONTRACTS LAW LECTURE NOTES

MUTUAL ASSENT (cont.)

- **The Acceptance**

    - **Unilateral Contracts: The Doing of the** **Act**
    - **Restatement 2d Rule: The Offeree's Choice**
    - **Bilateral Contracts: The Return Promise**
    - **Requirement of Unqualified Assent**
    - **When Acceptance is Effective**
        - **Acceptance by Unauthorized Means**
        - **What Constitutes Receipt**

    - **Rejection Sent Prior to Acceptance**
    - **Rejection Sent After Acceptance**

    - **Special Problems of Offer and Acceptance**
        - **Acceptance by Silence**
        - **The Written Memorial**
        - **Rewards and other Public Offers**

CONSIDERATION

- **The Element of Bargain**
    - **Distinguished from Conditional Gift**
    - **Distinguished from "Past Consideration"**

- **The Requirement of Legal Sufficiency**

    - **In Unilateral Contracts: In General**

CONTRACTS LAW LECTURE NOTES

ENFORCEMENT OF GRATUITOUS PROMISE

CONTRACTS LAW LECTURE NOTES

- o **Special Applications of the Doctrine**
- **The Doctrine of Moral Obligation**

    - o **Promises to pay Barred Debts**
    - o **Promises to Pay for Past Gratuitous Services**

DEFENSES TO FORMATION

- **The Statute of Fraud**

    - o **Agreements Not to be Performed within One Year**
        - **Contracts for Fixed Term**
        - **Contracts for One Year**
        - **Contracts Without a Fixed Term**
        - **Lifetime Contracts**
        - **Effect of Full Performance by One Party**

    - o **Promises to Answer for Debt or Default of Another**
        - **The Scope of the Clause**
        - **The Main Purpose Doctrine**

    - o **Promises in Consideration of Marriage**
    - o **Contracts for the Sale of Property**
    - o **Contracts for the Sale of Goods**
    - o **The Sufficiency of the Memorandum**
    - o **Special Problems**
        - **Estoppel to Assert the Statute**
        - **Oral Rescission and Modifications**

- **Lack of Capacity**

CONTRACTS LAW LECTURE NOTES

- o **Infant's Contracts**
- o **Contracts of Mentally Disabled Persons**

- **Illegal Bargains**

UNIFORM COMMERCIAL CODE

- **Provisions Related to the Offer**
  - o **Section 2-305: Certain of Terms**
  - o **Section 2-205: Revocation by the Offeror**

- **Provisions Relating to the Acceptance**
  - o **Section 1-201: Communication of Acceptance**
  - o **Section 2-206: Method of Acceptance**
  - o **Section 2-207: The Qualified Acceptance**

- **Auction Sales**

- **Provisions Related to Consideration**
  - o **Section 2-209: Modifications and Rescissions**
  - o **Sections 2-309 and 2-306: Illusory Promises**

- **Provisions Related Defenses to Formation**
  - o **Section 2-201: The Statute of Frauds**
  - o **Section 2-302: Unconscionable Contracts**

CONTRACTS LAW LECTURE NOTES

THE PAROL EVIDENCE RULE

- **Statement of the Rule**
  - The Integrated Contract
  - Change in Terms by Contradiction
  - Change in Terms by Additional Provisions

- **Exceptions to the Rule**

BREACH OF CONTRACT

- **Introduction**

- **Non-performance by Defendant**

  - Issues re Implied Terms
  - Prospective Nonperformance: Anticipatory Breach
    - Express and Implied Repudiation
    - Legal Effect of Anticipatory Breach
    - Limitations on the Doctrine
      - Plaintiff's Waiver of the Breach
      - Retraction of the Repudiation
      - Contracts Fully Performed by Plaintiff

- **Legal Excuses for Defendant's Nonperformance**

  - Failure of Condition

CONTRACTS LAW LECTURE NOTES

- - Conditions Defined
  - What constitutes a Material Failure
    - Express Conditions
    - Implied in Fact Conditions
    - Constructive Conditions

  - Problems re Plaintiff's Partial Performance
    - Substantial Performance
    - Conditions re Time of Performance
    - Conditions re Satisfaction
    - Conditions in Divisible Contracts

  - Excuse of Conditions
    - Waiver by Defendant
    - Prior Material Default by Defendant
    - Impossibility of Performing the Condition
  - Prospective Failure of Condition

- Termination of the Contract

  - By Agreement of the Parties

    - Mutual Rescission
    - Release
    - Novation
    - Accord and Satisfaction
    -
  - By Operation of Law

CONTRACTS LAW LECTURE NOTES

- Impossibility of Performance
- Impracticability of Performance
- Frustration of Purpose

- **Legal Effect of a Breach of Contract**

  - Material and Minor Breach Distinguished
  - Election to Treat Material Breach as Minor
  - Breach of Contracts for the Sale of Goods

- **Damages**

  - In General
  - Consequential Damages
  - Duty to Mitigate Damages
  - Specific Application of Damages Rules
    - Employment Contracts
    - Construction Contracts
    - Sales Contracts
  - Liquidated Damages Provisions

THIRD PARTY BENEFICIARIES

- **Standing to Sue as an Intended Beneficiary**
  - No Obligation Intended: Incidental Beneficiary
  - Intended Beneficiary
    - Satisfaction of an Obligation
    - Conferring of a Benefit

CONTRACTS LAW LECTURE NOTES

- **Validity of the Third Party Beneficiary Contract**
  - ○ **Breach by the Promisor**
    - ▪ **Legal Excuse of Failure of Conditions**
    - ▪ **Legal Excuse of Termination: Vesting of Rights**

- **Rights of Beneficiary Against the Promisee**

- **Rights of Promisee Against the Promisor**

ASSIGNMENT OF RIGHTS

- **Standing to Sue as an Assignee**

  - ○ **Existence of a Valid Contract**
  - ○ **Assignability of the Right**
    - ▪ **Personal Rights**
    - ▪ **Contractual Provisions Against Assignment**
    - ▪ **Statutory Provisions Against Assignment**
    - ▪ **Partial Assignments**
  - ○ **Validity of the Transfer**

- **Problems Relating to the Obligor's Breach**

  - ○ **Failure of Conditions**
  - ○ **Termination of the Contract**
  - ○ **Setoffs**

- **Special Problems re Assignments**

CONTRACTS LAW LECTURE NOTES

- o **Revocation of Gratuitous Assignments**
- o **Rights of Successive Assignees**
- o **Warranties of the Assignor**

DELEGATION AND ASSUMPTION OF DUTIES

- **The Elements of a Valid Delegation**
  - o **Personal v. Impersonal Duties**
  - o **How Delegation is Made**

- **Assumption of Duties**

- **Rights and Duties of the Assingor/Delegator**

CONTRACTS LAW LECTURE NOTES

CHAPTER 1- Contract Formation

Definition of a Contract

A voluntary and legally binding agreement between 2 or more parties.

Disputes or issues related to broken promises:

Has a valid contract been formed?

- Are the ELEMENTS of a contract present?
- Are there are DEFENSES to formation?

ELEMENTS of a Contract

- Mutual Assent, and
- Consideration

What is MUTUAL ASSENT?

- Requirement of an initial AGREEMENT between the parties to enter into a contractual relationship and to the terms of the proposed transaction.

Elements of MUTUAL ASSENT. The rules of OFFER and ACCEPTANCE.

CONTRACTS LAW LECTURE NOTES

- A valid OFFER has been made by one party,

- A valid ACCEPTANCE has been given by the other, and

Page | 12

- The acceptance has become effective PRIOR to the TERMINATION of the offer.

The OFFER

An OFFER is a PROMISE to carry out the terms of a proposed transaction which BARGAINS for an act, forbearance, or return promise to be given in exchange.

Is there a good & valid OFFER?

1. Is there a PROMISE?

2. Does the promise BARGAIN for something in exchange?

3. Are there any problems as to the TERMS of the OFFER?

   a. Are the terms sufficiently DEFINITE AND CERTAIN?
   b. Are there problems of MISTAKE OR AMBIGUITY?

CONTRACTS LAW LECTURE NOTES

4. Are there any problems of COMMUNICATION of the OFFER?

Is there a PROMISE?

There must be words or conduct on the part of the offeror which can reasonably be interpreted as a manifestation of PRESENT COMMITMENT, subject only to the offeree's assent.

The existence of a promise is tested by the objective theory. The test is the REASONABLE BELIEF of the offeree. The actual intent of the offeror is <u>not</u> controlling.

IMPLIED PROMISE

A promise may be expressed in words or inferred from conduct.

Advertisement and Circulars

<u>General rule</u>, advertisement and circulars offering items for sale are construed to be invitations to potential customers and do NOT manifest present contractual intent.

Quotations of Price

CONTRACTS LAW LECTURE NOTES

If quoting the price is the <u>initial</u> communication between the parties, it would not generally be construed as an offer.   But, if the quote is <u>in response</u> to an inquiry, it is more likely that it will be construed as a PROMISE to sell at that price.

Use of the word "offer"

The use of the word "offer" by one party does not necessarily mean that the communication will be given that legal effect.

Effect of Setting a Time Limit

Where the party making the proposal gives the other a certain period of time in which to communicate an answer, this is some evidence that an OFFER is intended.

COUNTER-OFFER

A counteroffer is an offer by the original offeree regarding the same transaction but containing terms which differ from those proposed in the original offer.

A counteroffer is merely an offer originating with the offeree, it is subject to all the rules applicable to offers in general.

CONTRACTS LAW LECTURE NOTES

A counteroffer may also have the legal effect as a possible rejection of the original offer.

Does the promise BARGAIN for something in exchange?

BARGAIN: distinguished from <u>gratuitous promise</u>. The offeror must be asking for something in exchange for his promise. If the person making the promise does not bargain for something in exchange, he is making a gratuitous promise rather than an offer.

Enforcement of gratuitous promise is not dealt with on the basis of the offer and acceptance rules here.

Are there any problems as to the TERMS of the offer?

Certainty of Terms:

In order for a valid contract to be formed, the essential terms must be sufficiently DEFINITE and CERTAIN to enable a court to determine the existence of a breach and to affix damages.

If an offer does not contain the essential terms AND if it is not one which is capable of being made certain by the acceptance or by reference to other

CONTRACTS LAW LECTURE NOTES

circumstances, it will not form the basis of a valid contract.

Contracts for Sale of Land: Subject matter of the sale must be described with reasonable certainty. The PRICE to be paid must be set out in the contract or must be capable of being ascertained by reference to some outside source.

Where the parties provide that the price is to be agreed upon in the future, the contract fails for uncertainty if they fail to agree.

Contracts for Sale of Goods- The Uniform Commercial Code (UCC) allows for more indefiniteness of terms, and also provides that the contract can be based on a reasonable price even where the parties fail to agree.

Construction and Repair Contracts- The work to be done must be described with reasonable certainty. The price must be set out or ascertainable by reference to some outside source.

Employment contracts- Type & length of employment and the salary to be paid must be described with reasonable certainty.

CONTRACTS LAW LECTURE NOTES

Mistake or Ambiguity in the Terms of the Contract

Mistake- a mistake in the offer may prevent the formation of a contract or it may give one party grounds for rescinding a contract which has been formed.

Mistake by an Intermediary-

Intermediary is Agent of Offeror- mistake by an agent of the offeror has the same legal effect as if made by the offeror himself.

Independent Intermediary

One view: the one choosing the intermediary is responsible for its mistakes if the other party had no reason to know of the mistake.

Other view: the offeror is not responsible for the mistake of the independent intermediary. Thus, no contract would be formed.

Mistake as Grounds to Rescind Contracts

If Offeror makes a mistake in his offer, and Offeree does have reason to know about the mistake, then the offeror has grounds to rescind the contract. If offeree has no reason to know about the mistake, offeror cannot rescind contract on basis of mistake.

CONTRACTS LAW LECTURE NOTES

Ambiguity in Terms

Ambiguity in an offer arises where a term of the offer is susceptible to more than one interpretation. In some circumstances, ambiguity may prevent the formation of a contract.

Where both parties have reason to know of the ambiguity, there is NO contract unless both parties have given the ambiguity term the same interpretation.

Where neither party has reason to know of the ambiguity, there is no contract unless both parties have given the ambiguous term the same interpretation.

Where one party has reason to know of the ambiguity and the other does not, there is a contract according to the interpretation of the "innocent party", i.e., the party who does not know about the ambiguity.

Communication of the Offer

An Offer must be communicated.

Communication takes place when the offeree has received and is aware of the offer. Mere receipt of

CONTRACTS LAW LECTURE NOTES

the offer, standing alone, is not sufficient to give the offeree the power of acceptance.

Termination of the Offer

In order to form a valid contract, an acceptance must take effect PRIOR to the termination of the offer.

The exact point at which the offer terminates is very important.

An offer may terminate by any one of the following means:

- **Lapse of time**
- **Revocation by the offeror**
- **Rejection by the offeree**
- **Death or insanity of the offeror**
- **Destruction of the subject matter of the contract, or the enactment of the legislation making the contract illegal**

Termination by Lapse of Time

An offer will terminate at the expiration of the time limit set in the offer or, if no time limit is given, within a reasonable time.

CONTRACTS LAW LECTURE NOTES

Issues related to Lapse of Time:

- Is there a specific time limit stated in the offer?

  - When does it begin to run?
  - Is there a problem as to delay in receipt?

- In the absence of a specific time limit, what might be considered a reasonable time?

- What is the effect of a late acceptance?

Is there a specific time limit stated in the offer?

Where the offeror states in his offer that the offer will expire on a certain date, the acceptance MUST take effect prior to the expiration of that time limit.

When does the time limit being to run?

Effect of Delay in Receipt of the Offer.

In the absence of a set time limit, the offer terminates within a reasonable time.

What constitutes a <u>reasonable time</u> is a question of fact which must be determined on the basis of all of the circumstances.

CONTRACTS LAW LECTURE NOTES

Effect of a Late Acceptance- an acceptance after the offer has been terminated operates as a COUNTEROFFER. If offeror desires to form a contract, the offeror must communicate his acceptance of the counteroffer to the offeree.

Revocation by the Offeror

A revocation is a manifestation by the offeror that he no longer intends to enter into the proposed contract.

Issues related to revocation:

- Does the offeror have the power to revoke?
- When does the revocation become effective?
- Is there an issue of indirect revocation?
- Is there an issue re revocation of an offer for a unilateral contract?

A revocation becomes effective upon its receipt by the offeree. A revocation is deemed to be received when it comes into the possession of the offeree or his agent, or when it is deposited in a customary or authorized place for the receipt of this type of communication. A revocation may be effective even though the offeree is unaware of its receipt. (Minority View- revocation effective when sent by offeror)

CONTRACTS LAW LECTURE NOTES

Is there an Indirect Revocation?

An indirect revocation occurs when the offeror takes **DEFINITE ACTION** inconsistent with an intention to enter into the proposed contract, **AND** the offeree acquires **RELIABLE INFORMATION** to that effect before making an acceptance.

Unilateral contracts- Revocation issue?

Certain offers bargain for the <u>DOING OF AN ACT</u> by the offeree, thus contemplating the formation of a unilateral contract.   Here, <u>performing of the requested act constitutes acceptance</u>.

<u>Instantaneous Acts</u>- if the act is one which can be performed instantaneously, the offeror can revoke his offer at any time **PRIOR** to **PERFORMANCE** by the offeree.

<u>Acts Requiring a Period of Time</u>- If an act is one which takes a period of time and the offeree has embarked upon performance.   Can the offeror thereafter revoke?

Two conflicting views:

<u>Strict view</u>- Offeror's revocation will be effective if it is received by offeree prior to the time offeree

CONTRACTS LAW LECTURE NOTES

has accepted (i.e., giving FULL PERFORMANCE) of the specified act.

Other view- Offeror cannot revoke his offer once offeree has embarked upon performance. As long as offeree is willing to complete the specified act, offeror is bound by the terms of his offer.

For the offer to be irrevocable under this view, the offeree must do more than merely PREPARE to enter upon performance.

He must have in fact embarked upon or at least tendered his performance of the requested act prior to the offeror's attempt to revoke.

Rejection by the Offeree

A <u>rejection</u> is a manifestation by the offeree that he does not intend to accept the offer or give it further consideration.

Issues related to Rejection:

- Has the offeree expressly or impliedly manifested an intention to reject the offer?
- When does the rejection become effective?

Has the offeree expressly or impliedly manifested an intention to reject the offer?

CONTRACTS LAW LECTURE NOTES

The problem with implied rejects arises when the offeree responds to the original offer with an inquiry or proposal suggesting different terms.

A counteroffer, standing alone, constitutes an implied rejection of the original offer. Not every counteroffer is a rejection. A counteroffer merely carries with it an implication of a rejection. This implication can be overcome by any language which indicates that the offeree is still considering the original offer.

When does a rejection become effective?

A rejection becomes effective upon receipt by the offeror. A rejection is deemed to be received when it comes into the possession of the offeror or his agent, or when it is deposited in a customary or authorized place for the receipt of this type of communication.

Death or Insanity of Either Party

The death or insanity of the offeror prior to acceptance of the offer terminates the offer.
Two conflicting views:

1. Death or insanity of the offeror terminates the offer as of the time that it occurs and

communication to the offeree is not necessary.

2. Other view- as long as the offeree has received no notice of the death or insanity he still has the power to accept the offer.

<u>Death or insanity of the offeree</u> makes it impossible for him to accept the offer. No one else can accept on his behalf, and the offer will terminate by lapse of time.

<u>Destruction of subject matter or illegality of the proposed contract</u>
Where, prior to acceptance by the offeree, the subject matter of the contract is destroyed or the proposed contract becomes illegal, the offer is thereby terminated.

<u>ACCEPTANCE</u>

An ACCEPTANCE is an expression of assent by the offeree to the terms of the offer. The manner in which this asset is manifested depends upon the nature of the offer, i.e., whether the offeror is contemplating a <u>unilateral</u> or <u>bilateral contract</u>.

<u>Unilateral Contract</u>

Here, it is contemplated by the offeror that he shall not be bound by his offer until he has received

CONTRACTS LAW LECTURE NOTES

PERFORMANCE by the offeree (rather than a PROMISE of performance). The contract is unilateral since it imposes an obligation on only one party, the offeror.

Reverse Unilateral Contract- this type of contract involves complete performance by the offeror and a resulting obligation on the part of the offeree.

Bilateral contract

Here, it is contemplated by the offeror thtat the offeree shall make a return promise to give certain performance, and both parties are bound from the time that the offeree's promise is given. The contract is bilateral since it imposes obligations on both sides.

Issues related to Acceptance

- If the offeror is contemplating a unilateral contract, has the offeree given the requested performance with knowledge of the offer and with intent to accept it?

- If the offeror is contemplating a bilateral contract:

  o Has the offeree given the requested return promise?

CONTRACTS LAW LECTURE NOTES

- o Was the return promise an <u>unqualified assent</u> to the terms of the offer?

- o At what point did the acceptance <u>become effective?</u>

<u>In a proposed unilateral contract, has the offeree given the requested performance with knowledge of the offer and with intent to accept?</u>

<u>Traditional view</u>: Offeree can only accept by actually giving the performance requested. A mere promise to perform does not constitute an acceptance.

<u>Modern view</u>: where no manner of acceptance is insisted upon, the offeree can choose between an acceptance by performance or an acceptance by a promise. Under this view, if the offeree chooses to perform the act, this beginning to perform creates an obligation to complete performance.

<u>Knowledge and Intent to Accept</u>- performance by the offeree of the specified act does not in and of itself constitutes an acceptance. It is required that the act be performed with knowledge of the offer and with intent to accept it.

CONTRACTS LAW LECTURE NOTES

Must Notice of Performance be Given to the Offeror?

The general rule is the offeree is under <u>no duty to notify</u> the offeror that he has performed the requested act.

But, if an offeree has reason to know that the offeror has no adequate means of promptly learning that the act has been performed, the offeree must exercise <u>reasonable diligence</u> to notify the offeror.

Acceptance of an offer for a bilateral contract

Where the offer is for a bilateral contract, the offeree accepts by giving a **PROMISE** of performance in accordance with the terms of the offer. This promise is manifested in the form of a **RETURN COMMUNICATION** from the offeree indicating his assent to the offer.

Manifesting a Promise by Doing an Act

Performance as a Substitute for a Promise

Unless the offer clearly indicates to the contrary, full performance by the offeree is an **ACCEPTABLE SUBSTITUTE** for the given of a promise. If the offeree chooses to render performance, his

CONTRACTS LAW LECTURE NOTES

beginning to perform operates as a promise to complete performance.

Was RETURN PROMISE an unqualified assent to the terms of the offer?

The acceptance must be <u>unqualified</u>. A return promise by the offeree must constitute an unqualified assent to the terms of the offer. If the offeree purports to accept but makes the acceptance conditional upon different terms, the purported acceptance operates as a counteroffer.

A mere suggestion or inquiry concerning more favorable terms does not make an acceptance a counteroffer.

Terms "<u>inherent in the offer</u>"- terms which are inherent in the offer even though not expressly stated. In cases where the offeree will purpose to make his acceptance conditional upon one of these inherent terms. This does not make the acceptance condition. Offeree is not really asking for different terms.

When does an acceptance become effective
An acceptance is effective when it is <u>communicated</u> to the offeror. When the parties are dealing in face-to-face transaction or over the telephone,

CONTRACTS LAW LECTURE NOTES

ACTUAL COMMUNICATION of the acceptance is required.

Where the parties are dealing at a distance by means of written communications, the prevailing rule is, acceptance which is transmitted by <u>authorized means</u> takes effect as soon as it is put of the offeree's possession, whether or not the acceptance ever reaches the offeror.

<u>Authorized Means</u>

Any means requested or suggested by the offeror in his offer. Where no means designated, communicated by the same means used by the offeror.

<u>Other Customer Means</u>- any means which would be considered customary in the particular type of transaction; a means which is as fast as or faster than that used by the offeror.

<u>Effect of an Acceptance by Unauthorized Means</u>

If acceptance is sent by other than authorized means, than most courts hold that acceptance becomes effective <u>upon receipt</u> and would complete the contract at that time unless the offer has previously terminated.

CONTRACTS LAW LECTURE NOTES

Other views hold that acceptance in such case would be effective <u>when sent</u>, provided that it is received within the time a properly dispatched acceptance would normally have been received.

<u>Receipt of Acceptance</u>- an acceptance is deemed received when it <u>comes into the possession</u> of the offeror or his agent, or when it is <u>deposited in a customary or authorized</u> place for the receipt of this type of communication.

<u>Effect of a Rejection Sent Prior to an Acceptance</u>
The general rule is once the offeree sends a rejection of the offer and then sends a subsequent acceptance, the acceptance will not be effective <u>until received</u>. Whether the acceptance will complete the contract when received will depend on whether the offer is still open at that time.

<u>Effect of a Rejection Sent after an Acceptance, but Received First</u>

The rule is that if the offeror <u>changes his position</u> in reliance upon the rejection, the offeree is stopped from asserting that there is in fact a contract.

CONTRACTS LAW LECTURE NOTES

Acceptance by Silence

In general, mere silence will not operate to impose contractual obligation. In the following situations, silence will operate as an acceptance of an offer:

- Where the offer so provides
- Failure to reject offered goods or services
- Previous dealings between the parties

Does a Written Memorial have the same effect as a formal contract?

In the absence of a clear intent to the contrary, the courts tend to favor the interpretation that the parties intended the formation of a contract at the time that their informal agreement was reached and that the contemplated formal document was to be merely a "memorial of the transaction".

But, if it clearly appears that the parties considered the signing of the document as the act which would give rise to contractual liability, no contract would be formed until both parties have signed.

Public Offers and Rewards

A public offer is one which is directed to the public in general, or a segment of the public, rather than to an individual.

CONTRACTS LAW LECTURE NOTES

Acceptance of a Public Offer

A public offer is unilateral in nature and is accepted by completing performance of the requested act with knowledge of the offer and with intent to accept it. A mere promise to perform would be ineffective.

Reward Cases

Performance by the offeree does not constitute acceptance unless he knows of the offer at the time.

If any part of the performance is rendered with knowledge of the offer and with intent to accept, there has been a valid acceptance.

Some courts have ruled that the right of the person claiming the reward should not depend on whether he knew of the offer at the time he performed the act, since the one offering the reward is gaining the same benefit in any event.

Revocation of a Public Offer

The offeror of a public offer may revoke it by publishing notice of revocation in the same manner as the original offer or in any other manner that is

CONTRACTS LAW LECTURE NOTES

designed to give the revocation equal publicity and reach the same segment of the public.

CONTRACTS LAW LECTURE NOTES

CHAPTER 2- Consideration

CONSIDERATION

Issues related to Consideration

- Has the promissory bargained for and received something in exchange for his promise?

- Is that which is bargained for and given in exchange legally sufficient consideration in terms of legal detriment to one or both promises? Is the benefit theory applicable?
- Do the facts raise issues with regard to special problems of consideration?
  - Is the promise forbearing to sue on an invalid claim?
  - Is there an attempted modification of a prior contract?
  - Is there a payment of a lesser amount in discharge of a debt?
  - Is there an illusory promise problem?

To have a <u>contract</u>, the elements of <u>Mutual Assent</u> and <u>Consideration</u> must be present.

Consideration is that which is <u>bargained for</u> and given in <u>exchange for a promise</u>. It may be an act,

CONTRACTS LAW LECTURE NOTES

a forbearance to act, or a return promise on the part of the promisee.

Without consideration, or something that is bargained for, the promise would be considered a gratuitous promise. Gratuitous promises are generally not enforceable except in special circumstances, e.g., Promissory Estoppel, and Moral Obligation.

Legal Sufficiency of Consideration

The subject matter of the bargain must be SUFFICIENT in the eyes of the law.

Has the promisor bargained for and receiving something in exchange for his promise?

Bargain

A promisor is said to be "bargaining" when he manifests an intention to be bound by a contractual obligation on CONDITION that he receives a certain thing in exchange.

Every offer includes within it the element of bargain. Once an offer has been made, the requirement of bargain is necessarily satisfied.

Bargain Distinguished from Conditional Gift

CONTRACTS LAW LECTURE NOTES

Whether the transaction is a mere promise to make a conditional gift or a bargain for a contract turns upon the promisor's apparent intent. Is it more consistent with a contracting or a donating state of mind?

Bargain Distinguished from Past Consideration

Where the promisor purports to give his promise in exchange for something which he has already received from the promise, there is no "bargain".

The promisor is NOT bound until he receives that which he has bargained for. No amount of preparation to perform on the part of the promise will act as consideration to support the promisor's promise.

Is that which is bargained for and given in exchange legally sufficient consideration?

Legally Sufficient in a Unilateral Contract

The general rule is the giving of the requested performance in a unilateral contract (perform an act or forbearance) situation is NOT legally sufficient consideration unless it involves a LEGAL DETRIMENT to the promisee.

CONTRACTS LAW LECTURE NOTES

Legal Detriment

Legal detriment means that the promisee is doing something which he was <u>not previously obligated</u> to do, or is giving up a <u>legal right</u>.

If the promisee is under a <u>pre-existing duty</u> to do or forbear doing a certain act, this performance in this regard does NOT constitute a legal detriment and is NOT legally sufficient consideration.

A <u>pre-existing duty may arise</u> by reasons of (1) an obligation imposed by law, (2) a prior contract with this same promisor, or (3) a prior contract with a third party.

<u>Pre-existing Duty: a Prior Contract with Same Promisor.</u> The traditional rule is that the giving of the same performance is NOT legally sufficient consideration to support an additional obligation on the part of the promisor.

<u>Pre-existing Duty: A prior Contract with a Third Party.</u> The general rule is that the giving of the same performance is NOT legally sufficient consideration to support an obligation on the part of the new promisor.

The "Benefit Theory" of Consideration

CONTRACTS LAW LECTURE NOTES

Legally Sufficient Consideration in a Bilateral Contract

A bilateral contract requires **MUTUAL OF OBLIGATION**, i.e., the contract must impose an obligation on BOTH parties. If one party is not bound, the entire contract fails.

How is MUTUAL OF OBLIGATION established?
It must appear that each promisee has incurred a legal detriment. If one promisee does not incur a legal detriment, there is no consideration for the other party's promise and therefore it is not binding upon him.

Legal Detriment in Bilateral Contracts
Each promisee is PROMISING to do something which he was not previously obligated to do, or is PROMISING to give a legal right.

In bilateral contracts- each party is both a promisor and a promisee. The rules of consideration require legal detriment to the PROMISEE.

When is LEGAL DETRIMENT lacking?
- The promisee is under a PRE-EXISTING DUTY to do that which he is now promising to do, or
- The promisee's promise is illusory

CONTRACTS LAW LECTURE NOTES

An illusory promise is one which by its terms imposes no obligation upon the person making it, and for that reason it does not constitute a legal detriment. So, if one of the parties to a bilateral contract has made an illusory promise, there is no mutuality of obligation and the entire contract fails.

Special Problems with Regard to Legal Sufficiency of Consideration in Unilateral and Bilateral Contracts:

- **Forbearance to Sue on an Invalid Claim**
  The general rule is the promisee's forbearance is sufficient if he HONESTLY believes that he has a valid claim.

- **Modification of a Prior Contract**
  The general rule is a modification must be supported by a NEW consideration. Other view (Restatement 2d) provides that a modification is binding without consideration if it is FAIR and EQUITABLE in view of the changed circumstances, or if there has been a material change of position in reliance on the new terms, or to the extend provided by the statute.

What is NEW consideration?

CONTRACTS LAW LECTURE NOTES

This means that the promisor is bargaining for and receiving something different from that which was promised him in the prior contract. Any change in the promisee's performance, no matter how slight, will constitute a sufficient legal detriment to support the modification.

Termination of the Prior Contract

If the prior contract has been terminated, neither party is thereafter under a pre-existing duty and each is free to negotiate a new contract on the same or different terms.

Methods of Terminating Prior Contract

- <u>Rescission</u>- the parties to a contract may **RESCIND** by mutual agreement, thereby terminating their obligations. A new contract entered into after the rescission would be supported by consideration even though performance by the promisee is the same as that promised in the prior agreement.

  <u>Commercial Impracticability</u>- where unforeseen difficulties increase the cost of performance **FAR OUT OF PROPORTION** to the price agreed upon in the original contract, the extreme impracticability of completing performance operates as a <u>DISCHARGE</u> of the

CONTRACTS LAW LECTURE NOTES

promisee's duty. The parties are thereafter free to negotiate a NEW contract.

COMPROMISE OF A DISPUTE: ACCORD

Where the validity of the contract or the amount owing is the subject of a GOOD FAITH DISPUTE, a compromise of that dispute is called an ACCORD agreement. Such an agreement is supported by consideration in that each party is giving up his LEGAL RIGHT to litigate the merits of the case.

Waiver of Provisions in the Contract:

Attempts to change the terms of a contract may take the form of a "waiver" by one party of some aspect of performance by the other party. Under certain circumstances, these "waivers" are binding without consideration.

Payment of a Lesser Amount in Discharge of a Debt

The general rule (the rule of Foakes v. Beer): a promise to accept a lesser amount in full payment of a debt is NOT binding upon the promisor unless it is supported by NEW consideration.

New consideration involves something different from that which the promisee is already obligated to give.

CONTRACTS LAW LECTURE NOTES

Qualifications to the General Rule

- Payment of a disputed or unliquidated claim. A claim is a disputed claim when its validity is not conceded by both parties. An unliquidated claim is one wherein the amount owing has not been definitely fixed by agreement, as where an attorney renders services for a client without fixing the fee in advance.

- The rule is that ANY amount which is tendered and accepted as FULL PAYMENT of a disputed or unliquidated claim operates as a discharge of the claim.

Release or "gift" by the Creditor: A release is a formal document discharging an existing obligation, and in some jurisdictions is valid WITHOUT consideration. So, a release given by the creditor on part payment by the debtor would operate as a discharge of the balance.

Illusory Promise

An illusory promise is one which by its terms imposes no obligation upon the party making it. It is where the terms of the contract give to one party an option of nonperformance that an issue of illusory promise is created. The specific problems in this area usually relate to (1) cancellation provision, and (2) requirement and output contracts.

- **Cancellation Provisions-**

  In general, where one party to a bilateral contract has the <u>unrestricted power of cancellation</u>, his promise of performance is illusory and does not impose a legal detriment upon him. A <u>power of cancellation</u> is considered unrestricted where it can be exercised at the whim of the party and no notice of cancellation is required.

- **Requirement and Output Contracts-**

  <u>Requirement Contract</u>- one wherein the buyer agrees to buy all of his requirements of a certain product from one particular seller.

  <u>Output contract</u>-one where the seller agrees to sell to one particular buyer ALL that he produces of a certain product. The rules of consideration applicable to output contracts are the same as those applied to requirement contracts.

  So long as the buyer does not have the alternative of buying elsewhere and the seller does not the alternative of selling elsewhere, they incurred a legal detriment and their promises are not made illusory.

CONTRACTS LAW LECTURE NOTES

Enforcement of Gratuitous Promises

The general rule is a gratuitous promise is <u>unenforceable</u>. Circumstances where gratuitous promises are permitted to be enforced:

- **Promissory Estoppel, and**
- **Moral Obligation**

Promissory Estoppel

This doctrine proceeds upon the general principle that under certain circumstances involving foreseeable detrimental reliance upon a gratuitous promise, a remedy against the non-performing promisor may be necessary in order to avoid injustice in the particular case.

A promise is binding upon the promisor under these circumstances:

1) The promise is one which the promisor should <u>reasonably expect</u> to induce action or forbearance on the part of the promisee or a third person;
2) The promise does in fact induce such action nor forbearance; and
3) Injustice can be avoided only be enforcement of the promise.

Where all these elements are present, a gratuitous promise will be enforceable as any valid contract. However, remedies for breach of such promise will be limited as justice requires.

Elements of Promissory Estoppel

<u>Detrimental Reliance</u>- In order to hold the promisor to his gratuitous promise, the promisee (or third person) must be induced to CHANGE HIS POSITION by reason of the promise. The change of position must be one which works a HARDSHIP upon the promisee to the extent that it would be UNFAIR to permit the promise to repudiate his promise.

Reasonable Foreseeability

It must also appear that it was reasonably foreseeable to the promisor that the promisee would be induced to act in this manner. If the promisor has no reason to foresee that the promisee will be induced to act in the particular manner, there is no basis for applying promissory estoppels.

Reliance by a Third Person

If detrimental reliance by the third party is foreseeable by the promissory, the promisorry

CONTRACTS LAW LECTURE NOTES

estoppels doctrine is applicable to the same extent as in the case of reliance by the promisee.

Partial Enforcement

Page | 47

This is where remedy for the promisor's breach may be limited as justice requires.

Promissory Estoppel in Bargain Situations

Bids by Contractors-
Promises of Franchises

The __Doctrine of Moral Obligation__- applied in 2 situations:

1) Where a debtor promises to pay a debt which has been barred by the Statute of Limitations or discharged in bankruptcy
2) Where a person promises to pay for gratuitous services previously rendered.

Promises to Pay an Expired Debt

In general, a NEW PROMISE to pay an antecedent debt which is barred by the Statute of Limitations is enforceable without a new consideration.

CONTRACTS LAW LECTURE NOTES

A new promise to pay:

Page | 48

- An express promise to pay
- An unqualified acknowledgement of a debt carries an implied promise to pay it. But if acknowledgement is qualified with a refusal or statement of inability to pay, no new promise can be implied.
- Part payment is an implied promise to pay the balance, unless it is asserted that partial payment is in full, or as a gratuity.
- Effect of a new promise prior to the running of the statute of limitations- the new promise extends the creditor's cause of action for another statutory period running from the date of the new promise.

A new promise to pay by one whose debt has been discharged in bankruptcy is enforceable without a new consideration. Here, a mere acknowledgement or part payment does NOT operate to create a new obligation on the part of the bankrupt.

Promises to Pay for Past Gratuitous Services

A promise to pay for something which has already been received by the promisor is generally not enforceable since the requisite element of bargain is lacking.

CONTRACTS LAW LECTURE NOTES

(Restatement position: promises made in recognition of a benefit previously received by the promisor are binding if the promisee conferred the benefit as a gift).

CONTRACTS LAW LECTURE NOTES

Chapter 3- Parol Evidence Rule

THE PAROL EVIDENCE RULE

This rule governs the circumstances under which evidence can be introduced to CHANGE <u>THE TERMS of a written contract</u>. It applies to other formal documents, such as deeds, wills and trust instruments.

<u>Statement of the Rule</u>- where the parties have reduced their agreement to a writing which is intended to represent a <u>FINAL and COMPLETE</u> expression of their contract, no evidence of prior or contemporaneous agreements can be introduced to <u>change the terms</u> of the writing.

<u>Parol Evidence Issues</u>

- Is there a written agreement intended to represent a final and complete contract between the parties?

- Is evidence of a prior or contemporaneous agreement being offered by one party to change the terms of the written contract?

    o Is the agreement prior or contemporaneous, as opposed to a subsequent modification?

- o Does it change the terms of the writing? If it contradicts the writing, it is inadmissible. If it adds to the writing, does the collateral agreement doctrine apply?

- Is the evidence being offered for some purpose which does not violate the Parol Evidence Rule?

  - o Is it offered to show that no valid agreement has been entered into?

  - o Is it offered for the purpose of interpreting the agreement, and if so, is it admissible for that purpose?

Does the written agreement represent a final and complete contract (is it "integrated")?

Merger Clause- a provision in the contract to the effect that the writing contains the entire contract of the parties.

Presence of the merger clause conclusively establishes that the writing is integrated and that the parties did intend for the writing to be final and complete.

If no merger clause, conflicting rules:

- The Face of the Instrument Test- whether a writing is integrated must be determined

CONTRACTS LAW LECTURE NOTES

SOLELY by looking at the writing itself. If it appears to be final and complete on its face, then the writing must be held to be integrated without inquiry into surrounding circumstances that might show a different intent.

- **Collateral Agreement Doctrine:** here the court will look outside the written contract to determine if the additional terms in question do in fact relate to a "collateral" part of the transaction.

- **Intent of the Parties Test-** other courts have taken the position that the actual intent of the parties should always control on the question of integration. The court can inquire into all of the surrounding circumstances.

Is evidence of a prior or contemporaneous agreement being offered by one party to change the terms of the written contract?

Prior or Contemporaneous vs. Modification

Only evidence as to agreements made prior to or at the same time as the written contract will be excluded as inadmissible parol evidence. The rule DOES NOT apply to subsequent modifying the contract.

CONTRACTS LAW LECTURE NOTES

Change in Terms- Contradiction

Such evidence will be INADMISSIBLE.

Change in Terms- Additional Provisions

Traditional rule: parol evidence is NOT admissible for the purpose of ADDING to the terms of an integrated contract.

Collateral Agreement Doctrine: Exception to the Parol Evidence Rule. Here, the court may find that the additional terms were intended to relate to a collateral aspect of the basic transaction, in which case the evidence will NOT be excluded by the parol evidence rule.

Collateral agreement- one in which

- Does not contradict any express provision of the main agreement, and

- Might naturally be made as a separate agreement between the parties.

Is the evidence being offered for some purpose which does not violate the parol evidence rule?

Evidence negating a valid agreement-

Parol evidence is always admissible to prove that the written agreement is invalid or unenforceable.

Parol evidence is admissible to prove:

CONTRACTS LAW LECTURE NOTES

- That the contract was not intended to take effect until a certain condition has occurred, or

- That the contract was induced by mistake, misrepresentation, or other circumstances giving rise to grounds for rescission, or

- That it was lacking in consideration

Interpretation of Terms

In general, parol evidence rule does not exclude evidence which is otherwise admissible to resolve ambiguities and to explain the intended meaning of contractual terms.

> Special Meanings: if the language is clear on its face, evidence cannot be introduced to vary this plain meaning.
>
> > Exception: Local Meanings- a special meaning commonly accepted in a particular trade or community. Such a meaning may be shown by parol evidence.
> >
> > Broad Rule: parol evidence should be readily admissible to aid in determining the meaning that the parties intended should be given to the contractual

CONTRACTS LAW LECTURE NOTES

terms, without limitation to local or trade usage.

Parol Evidence in Contract for Sale of Goods (UCC Section 2-202)

1.<u>Contradictory terms</u>- exclude evidence of any prior or contemporaneous oral agreement to contradict the terms of a final written agreement- only ORAL agreements are excluded.

2. <u>Added terms</u>- permits parol evidence to prove alleged new terms unless they are a type which the parties would CERTAINLY HAVE INCLUDED in their written contract if they had intended to be bound by them.

3. <u>Interpretation of terms</u>- allows the use of parol evidence relating to trade usage or a course of dealing or performance between the parties to EXPLAIN the terms of their agreement.

CONTRACTS LAW LECTURE NOTES

Chapter 4- Uniform Commercial Code (UCC)

Sale of Goods

Purpose of the UCC is to bring the law of sales closer to the commercial expectation of the parties and those practices that are employed in the marketplace.

Section 2-204 provides the general rule for formation.

- A contract may be made in any manner sufficient to show agreement.

- Conduct by both parties which recognizes the existence of a contract is sufficient under this section. Cross-offers may be sufficient to form a contract even though the usual rules of offer and acceptance are not thereby complied with.

Offers

- **Certainty of Terms**
  - **Open Price Terms**

CONTRACTS LAW LECTURE NOTES

- o **Output and Requirement Contracts**

- o **Single or Several Deliveries**

- o **Successive Performances**

- o **Place of Delivery**

- o **Time for Delivery**

- o **Time for Payment**

Even if one or more terms are left open, a contract will not fail for indefiniteness if the parties have intended to make a contract and there is a reasonably certain basis for giving an appropriate remedy.

<u>Firm Offer</u>

Under common law rule, an irrevocable offer is not binding upon the offeror unless supported by consideration.

Under the UCC, a FIRM OFFER (irrevocable offer) made by a MERCHANT to buy or sell goods in a <u>signed writing</u> and contains an assurance that it will be held open. This offer is not revocable for lack of consideration during the time stated. If no time stated, the offer is <u>irrevocable for a reasonable time but not to exceed 3 months.</u>

<u>Merchant</u>: a person who deals in goods of the kind involved in the transaction or otherwise by his

CONTRACTS LAW LECTURE NOTES

occupation holds himself out as having knowledge or skill peculiar to the practices or goods involved in the transaction.

Acceptance

- **Communication of Acceptance**- an acceptance sent by unauthorized means, which is received within the time it would have arrived if properly sent, is considered effective UPON DISPATCH. Under the majority common law rule, such an acceptance would not be effective until received.

- **Method of Acceptance**- Unless there is a clear manifestation of intent to the contrary, an offer to make a contract shall be construed as <u>inviting acceptance in any manner and by any medium reasonable in the circumstances.</u>

   - Acceptance of Offers to buy goods for prompt or current shipment

   - Beginning performance: Notification

   - Acceptance by Shipment of Non-confirming goods

Additional Terms in an Acceptance

- **Acceptance or Counteroffer**

Unless the offeree makes his asset to the offer **EXPRESSLY CONDITIONAL** upon the new terms, a purported acceptance which proposes different or added terms will result in the formation of a contract according to the terms of the original offer.

New terms are considered as proposals for additions to the contract. If the transaction is NOT between merchants, the added terms will NOT become part of the contract unless the other party assents to them. As <u>between merchants, the added terms automatically become a part of the contract unless</u>

- The offeror has expressly limited acceptance to the terms of the offer, or

- The added terms materially alter the offer; or

- Notice of objection is given by the offeror within a reasonable time.

<u>Special problem- Battle of the Form</u>

Section 2-207(3) provides that <u>conduct by both parties which recognizes the existence of a contract</u> is sufficient to establish a contract for the sale of goods even though the writings of the parties do not otherwise establish a contract between them. In such case, the terms of the <u>contract consist of those terms upon which the</u>

CONTRACTS LAW LECTURE NOTES

writings of the parties AGREE. The remaining terms have not effect.

Auction Sales- An auctioneer merely invites bids. Each bid constitutes an offer, the acceptance taking place with the fall of the hammer. If a new bid is made while the hammer is falling, auctioneer, at his discretion, to reopen bidding or to declare the sale final at that time.

Bidder may withdraw his bid at any time prior to the hammer falls.

If an auction is WITH RESERVE, the auctioneer may withdraw the goods at any time. If it is WITHOUT RESERVE, the auctioneer may not withdraw the goods except in a case where no offer has been made within a reasonable time.

All auctions are with reserve unless stated to be without reserve.

Consideration- The rules are the same as common law, except

- Firm offers

- Modification, Rescissions and Waiver

    UCC made significant changes in this area.

Common law rule- a modification of a contract is NOT enforceable unless it is supported by

CONTRACTS LAW LECTURE NOTES

consideration, and modification or rescission can be done orally unless the contract as modified comes under the Statute of Frauds.

Changes to common law rules made by UCC (2-209)

1. Modification of a contract needs no consideration to be binding, subject to general good faith dealings. If one party appears to have taken unfair advantage of a superior bargaining position, the modification will not be upheld.

2. Oral modification/rescission- if a written agreement provides that it cannot be modified or rescinded except by a signed writing, then such a provision will be given effect.

- **Illusory Promises**

One which by its terms imposes no obligation to perform upon the promisor. Some promises are (not enforceable under common law) enforceable in contracts for the sale of goods because of terms imposed upon the parties by UCC.

> **Cancellation Provisions-** termination of a contract by one party requires that reasonable notice be received by the other party. An agreement dispensing with notification is invalid if its operation would

be unconscionable. The imposition of notice requirement to effect termination of the contract supplies the required legal detriment to prevent the promisor's promise from being illusory.

<u>Exclusive dealings</u>- to avoid illusory problem, UCC imposes upon the seller an obligation to use his best efforts to supply the goods and upon the agent an obligation to use his best efforts to promote their sale.

CONTRACTS LAW LECTURE NOTES

CHAPTER 5- Defenses to Formation

DEFENSES TO FORMATION

Statute of Frauds- A contract for the sale of goods for a price of $500 or more is not enforceable unless there is a sufficient memorandum signed by the party against whom enforcement is sought or be his authorized agent.

Sufficiency of Memorandum

A memorandum will not be insufficient by reason of the fact that it omits or incorrectly states a term of the contract. The only that term that must appear is the **QUANTITY.**   Even this term need not be accurately state, but recovery will be limited to the amount set forth.

Confirmation between Merchants

If one party sends written confirmation of the transaction which is not object to within 10 days after its receipt, such a writing is a sufficient memorandum against both parties.

CONTRACTS LAW LECTURE NOTES

Exception to the Statute of Frauds provisions

Under these circumstances, an oral contract for the sale of goods priced at $500 or more may nevertheless be enforced:

- **Specially manufactured goods** for the buyer, and sellers has substantially begun their manufacture or has made commitments for their procurement. (Common law excluded specially manufactured goods from the Statute of Frauds altogether)

Unconscionable contract or contractual provision

The parties shall be given an opportunity to present evidence as to the commercial setting, purpose and effect of the clause or contract in question.

If a provision is found to be unconscionable, the court has the option of refusing to enforce the entire contract, or of enforcing the contract but limiting the effect of the particular provision so as to avoid an unconscionable result.

CONTRACTS LAW LECTURE NOTES

Defense to Formation: Statute of Frauds

Even when both mutual assent and consideration are present, other circumstances may affect the validity of a contract.

Issues involving defenses to contract formation

- Is the contract an oral one or represented by an insufficient writing? This would raise an issue of <u>Statute of Frauds</u>.

- Does one of the parties to the contract <u>lack capacity</u> by reason of infancy or mental infirmity?

- Are the circumstances such as to indicate tha the parties making an illegal bargain?

- Has the defendant been induced to enter into the contract by <u>mistake, misrepresentation or duress</u>, thereby giving him the right of rescission?

STATUTE OF FRAUDS

Requires certain contracts to be in writing in order to be valid

Purpose of statute of frauds was to guard against fraud and perjury in contract actions by requiring that certain types of contracts be evidenced by a writing signed by the party to be charged.

CONTRACTS LAW LECTURE NOTES

When dealing with Statute of Frauds issues-consider these two aspects of the problem:

1) **Is the particular contract within the Statute?**

   a. A contract which by its terms is not to be performed within ONE YEAR from the making

   b. A promise to ANSWER FOR THE DEBT of default of another

   c. A contract for the SALE OF REAL PROPERTY

   d. A contract for the SALE OF GOODS of a value in excess of a certain amount

2. Can the contract be taken out of the Statute? A contract can be rendered enforceable by a sufficient memorandum signed by the defendant.

Contracts where terms are not to be performed within one year from the date of making the contract

Applicable only to Bilateral Contracts, i.e., wherein performance on ONE or BOTH sides cannot be completed within one year from the making of the contract.

When is a contract incapable of being performed within one year?

CONTRACTS LAW LECTURE NOTES

- **Contracts for a fixed term exceed one year**

- **Contracts for a one-year term**

- **Contracts which do not provided for a fixed term**

- **Lifetime contracts**

How is this type of contract taken out of the Statute of Frauds?

- **A sufficient memorandum in writing, or**

- **Full performance on the part of the plaintiff in this action**

Full performance by one party

General rule, full performance by one party will remove the contract from the operation of the Statute without regard to the length of time required for completion of performance by defendants.

Promises to answer for the debt or default of another

This falls within the Statute of Frauds only if there is an obligation of some third person, either already existing or subsequently to be created, which the promisor undertakes to be answerable for.

CONTRACTS LAW LECTURE NOTES

<u>"Answer for" a debt?</u> The promisor must pay if called upon to do so, but is entitle to reimbursement from the third person.

Promises made directly to the debtor to pay his debt to a third person are NOT within the statute.

<u>How to take this type of contract out of the statute?</u>

- **Sufficient memorandum in writing**

- **Main Purpose Doctrine**

<u>Main Purpose Doctrine</u>- where the consideration which the promisor receives in exchange for his promise to answer for the debt of another is desired by him mainly for his OWN PECUNIARY or BUSINESS ADVANTAGE, his promise is removed from the operation of the Statute.

<u>Promises in Consideration of Marriage</u>

General rule, any promise in consideration of marriage or promise of marriage other than mutual promises to marry, is within the Statute of Frauds.

<u>Mutual promises to marry</u> are not within this section of the statute, but might fall within the ONE-YEAR provision if not to be performed within one-year from the making of the contract.

CONTRACTS LAW LECTURE NOTES

<u>To take this contract out of the Statute of Frauds-</u>
sufficient memorandum

<u>Contracts for the Sale of Real Property</u>

In general, a contract for the sale or purchase of real property or any interest therein is within the Statute.

Take this type of contract out of the Statute-sufficient memorandum, or part-performance, if applicable.

<u>Contracts for the Sale of Goods Valued in Excess of a Certain Amount</u>

Prior to the UCC, Section 2- Uniform Sales Act- the Statute of Frauds applies if

- Contracts for sales of goods valued at $500 or more would not be enforceable unless

  o There was a sufficient memorandum signed by the party to be charged or his agent, or

  o Buyer accepted all or part of the goods or paid all or part of the purchase price.

<u>Sufficiency of the Memorandum</u>

The memorandum must contain <u>sufficient terms of the contract</u> and <u>signed</u> by the party to be charged or his authorized agent.

CONTRACTS LAW LECTURE NOTES

- Identity of the parties,

- Subject matter of the contract,

- The price to be paid, and

- Any additional special terms

- Must be described with reasonable certainty

Any signed writing is sufficient so long as acknowledges the contract and contains the essential terms.

The memorandum can consist of one or more writing- they can be taken together to form the necessary memorandum so long as they can be identified as relating to the same transaction.

Special Problems: Estoppel to Assert Statute of Frauds

If defendant, by his words or conduct, represents that he will perform his contract despite the fact that it is within the Statute and the plaintiff relies upon this assertion to his detriment, defendant will be stopped to assert the Statute in a later action brought by the plaintiff.

Detrimental Reliance- if not induced by a misrepresentation on the part of the defendant will NOT take the oral contract out of the statute.

CONTRACTS LAW LECTURE NOTES

Special Problem- Oral Rescission and Modifications

A written contract can be rescinded ORALLY whether or not it was required to be in writing by the Statute of Frauds. A written contract may also be modified orally unless the contract at this inception or as modified is covered by a Statute of Frauds provision.

Defense to Formation: Lack of Capacity

If one of the parties to the contract was an infant or suffering from a mental infirmity at the time of the contract was formed, he may be entitled to disaffirm the contract. Power of disaffirmance

Infant: a person who has not reached the age of majority. The common law age of majority is 21. A number of jurisdictions is 18.

Infant's Power of Disaffirmance: an infant's contract is deemed to be voidable, i.e., it is valid for all purposes unless and until it is disaffirmed by the infant.

Legal effect of disaffirmance- terminate the contract.

How is Power of Disaffirmance exercised

By manifesting to the other party an unwillingness to continue to be bound by the contract.

CONTRACTS LAW LECTURE NOTES

If the infant has received some benefits, e.g. goods, etc., he must return them once the contract is disaffirmed.

Infant must disaffirm <u>either before majority or within a reasonable time</u> thereafter.

New promise after reaching majority:

<u>Ratification</u>- after reaching majority, infant makes a <u>new promise to fulfill</u> the obligation or acts in such a manner that <u>an intention to recognize his obligation</u> can reasonably be inferred- the rule is this new promise, express or implied, operates as a <u>ratification</u> and the contract cannot thereafter be disaffirmed. No new consideration is needed.

<u>Quasi-contractual recovery for necessaries</u>-

The person providing the necessaries is entitled to quasi-contractual recovery. This recovery is measured by the reasonable value of the necessaries rather than the contract price.

<u>Defense to Formation: Mentally Disabled Persons</u>

<u>General rule</u>- a contract entered into by someone of unsound mind who has NOT been legally adjudicated insane is deemed to be VOIDABLE by him. If he has been legally adjudicated insane, such contract would be VOID.

CONTRACTS LAW LECTURE NOTES

Ratification of a voidable contract

Recovery for necessaries

Defense to Formation- Illegal Bargains

The contract is illegal and therefore VOID.

- **Contracts that are illegal at the outset**

- **Courts will not grant recovery to a plaintiff who is seeking to hold defendant liable for a breach or to a plaintiff who is seeking to "undo" the transaction and recover that which he has given.**

Examples of Illegal Bargains

Special problem- Licensing statutes

When will a <u>remedy</u> be given despite the illegal nature of the contract?

- **Partial illegality**

- **Recovery by a party who is not in pari delicto**

- <u>**Doctrine of "locus poenitentiae"**</u>**- a party who has rendered performance under an illegal contract may obtain restitution of that which he has given if:**

  - **The performance did not involve serious misconduct on his part, and**

- He withdraws from the transaction before the improper purpose has been achieved.

Special problem: Unconscionable Contracts or Contractual Provisions

If the contract is unconscionable (gross inequality of bargaining power), the court may refuse to enforce the contract or the particular term, or may limit the application of a particular term so as to avoid an unconscionable result.

A third party has standing to sue if he can qualify as an intended beneficiary of the promisor's performance.

Promisor may defeat the rights of the beneficiary by showing:

- That no valid contract was formed in the first instance, or

- That the promisor has a legal excuse for his non-performance

CONTRACTS LAW LECTURE NOTES

CHAPTER 6- Third Party Issues

<u>Third party beneficiaries issues:</u>

- **Does plaintiff have standing to sue as an intended beneficiary?**

    - ○ **Do the parties contemplate an obligation shall be created in favor of a third person?**

        - ▪ **Will performance by promisor satisfy an obligation owing by the promisee to the beneficiary?**

        - ▪ **If not, is it the intent of the promisee to give to the beneficiary the benefit of the promisor's performance?**

- **Is there a problem relating to the validity of the third party beneficiary contract?**

- **Is there a problem relating to the promisor's breach? If the promisor is asserting the legal excuse of termination or modification of the contract arising out an agreement with the promisee, have the beneficiary's rights <u>vested</u>?**

CONTRACTS LAW LECTURE NOTES

Does the plaintiff have standing to sue as an intended beneficiary?

- A third person is deemed to be an intended beneficiary if

    - Performance by the promisor will satisfy an obligation of the promisee to pay money to the beneficiary, or

    - The circumstances indicate that the promisee intends to give the beneficiary the benefit of the promisor's performance.

Intended Beneficiaries:

1. **Creditor beneficiary**- if no intent to make a gift appeared and performance by the promisor would satisfy an actual, supposed or asserted obligation owing by the promisee to the beneficiary.

2. **Donee beneficiary**- it it appeared that the intent of the promisee in obtaining the promisor's promise to perform to the beneficiary was to make a gift.

Satisfaction of the promisee's obligation (Creditor beneficiary)

CONTRACTS LAW LECTURE NOTES

Promised performance of the promisor will satisfy an obligation owing by the promisee to the beneficiary.

"Mixed" Beneficiary- regarded as a donee beneficiary.

Conferring a benefit (Donee beneficiary)

The intent of the promisee, in obtaining the promisor's promise to perform to the beneficiary, is to confer a gratuitous benefit upon the beneficiary.

In the absence of clear expression of intent, the promisee's desire to confer the benefit may be inferred from the circumstances surrounding the transaction.

Is there a problem relating to the validity of the third party beneficiary contract?

Validity of contract

A promisor may defeat a third party beneficiary action by showing that the alleged contract is lacking in mutual assent or consideration, or that his promise is unenforceable by reason of the Statute of Frauds, legal incapacity, illegality, or that there are grounds for rescission such as misrepresentation or mistake.

CONTRACTS LAW LECTURE NOTES

Is there a problem relating to the promisor's breach?

The rights of the third party beneficiary are dependent upon establishing a breach of contract on the part of the promisor. In this connection, the legal excuse of failure of condition or termination of the contract may be available to the promisor to defeat the beneficiary's cause of action.

Failure of Conditions

The law of express and constructive conditions is applicable to third party beneficiary contracts.

Termination of the Contract

Termination by operation of law, as in the case of impossibility of performance or frustration of purpose.

When the original parties to the contract want to terminate the third party beneficiary contract by agreement, mutual rescission, or attempt to modify the contract so as to impair the rights of the beneficiary.

The rule: unless the contract provices to the contrary, the original parties are entitled to terminate or modify the third party beneficiary contract at any point prior to the time that the beneficiary's rights have vested.

<u>When do the beneficiary's rights vest?</u>

Most courts hold that the rights of both the done and creditor vest upon the beneficiary's learning of the third party beneficiary contract and manifesting assent thereto.

<u>Restatement 2d Section 311 provides that:</u>

In the absence of a contrary agreement, the original parties retain the power to defeat or alter the beneficiary's rights.

This power ceases when the beneficiary, before receiving notification of the termination or modification

(1) Materially changes his position, including the bring of suit, or

(2) Manifests assent to the contract in a manner invited by the promisor or promisee.

<u>Material Change of Position</u>- an intended beneficiary who learns of the contract is ordinarily justified in relying on it. Any material change of position precludes a later attempt to terminate or alter his rights.

CONTRACTS LAW LECTURE NOTES

<u>Beneficiary's Assent</u>- If, after receiving notification of the contract from the promisor or the promisee, the beneficiary manifest assent thereto, this operates as a vesting of rights even in the absence of a change of position.

Page | 80

Rights of the third party beneficiary against the promisee

<u>Creditor Limited to Original Obligation</u>- a third party beneficiary contract does not give the creditor new rights against the promisee. Whatever prior rights the creditor had against the promisee by reason of the original obligation remain unaffected by the third party beneficiary contract.

<u>Donee has no rights</u>- where the promisee intends to confer a benefit upon the beneficiary in the nature of a gift, the beneficiary acquires no rights against the promisee by reason of the third party beneficiary contract. The promisee is under no obligation to perform to the beneficiary or to assure performance by the promisor.

Rights of the Promisee against the Promisor

<u>Creditor Situations</u>- where the promisor repudiates his obligation to discharge the debt of the promisee owing to the beneficiary, the promisee as well as the beneficiary can bring an action against the promisor. Recovery by either party will bar an action by the other.

CONTRACTS LAW LECTURE NOTES

<u>Donee Situations</u>- It is generally recognized that the remedy of specific performance is available to the promisee to compel the promisor to perform as agreed.

Assignment of Rights

An assignment is a transfer of a contractual right. An assignment is not a contract involving a promise to do something in the future, but is a <u>present transfer of property</u>.

The subject matter of the assignment consists of <u>INTANGIBLE PROPERTY</u>- a contractual right (also called a <u>chose in action</u>).

Rights distinguished from Duties

When one party has a right, the other party to the contract has a correlative duty.

Issues involving Assignments

- Does plaintiff have standing to sue as an assignee of a contractual right?

    - Does a valid contract exist between the original contracting parties, creating a right in favor of the assignor?

    - Was the right in question an assignable one?

    - Has the right been validly assigned?

CONTRACTS LAW LECTURE NOTES

- Are there problems relating to the obligor's breach? What legal excuses can be raised for the obligor's nonperformance?

- Are there problems relating to revocation of the assignment, successive assignments, or warranties by the assignor?

Does the third party have standing to sue as an assignee of a contractual right?

General: A valid assignment requires

- The existence of a valid contract creating the right in questions;

- A right which is capable of being assigned; and

- A valid transfer of that right by the assignor to the assignee

A valid existing contract

Existence of the contract at the time of Assignment

An attempted assignment of rights under a contract not yet in existence operates as a promise to assign. This promise, if supported by consideration, is actionable to the same extent as any other contractual promise and

CONTRACTS LAW LECTURE NOTES

in an appropriate case specific performance may be obtained.

<u>Assignability of the Right</u>

In general, a right under an existing contract may be assigned unless:

- It is too personal,
- Assignment is prohibited by the terms of the contract, or
- Assignment is prohibited by law

<u>Is the right too personal for assignment?</u>

A right is deemed to be a personal right if the relationship between the original contracting parties is such that it must have been contemplated that the obligor would be called upon to render performance only to the other contracting party.

<u>Right to receive money</u>- generally considered impersonal

<u>Right to services under an employment contract</u>- depends on nature of the services to be rendered. If the serves are of a personal nature, the right to receive such services cannot be transferred to a third person.

CONTRACTS LAW LECTURE NOTES

<u>Contracts for the Sale of Land</u>- generally, it does not materially vary the performance of the seller (so long as payment is forthcoming) if he is called upon to convey title to a third person rather than the original buyer.

<u>Contracts for the Sale of Goods</u>- (UCC Section 2-210) unless otherwise agreed, the rights of either the buyer or the seller can be assigned except where the assignment would materially change the duty of the other party or impair his chances of obtaining return performance.

<u>Requirement Contracts</u>-

Contractual Prohibitions Against Assignment

Under the UCC- Section 2-210

1. Unless the circumstances indicate to the contrary, a provision against assignment of the contract is to be construed as prohibiting only a delegation of duties. Since a prohibition against an assignment of rights is a restraint upon the transferability of property, such a prohibition will not be inferred.

2. Regardless of an agreement to the contrary, an assignor may assign a right to damages for breach of the entire contract or a right

created by the assignor's full performance of his side of the contract.

Statutory Prohibitions Against Assignment

Partial Assignments

Requirement of a Valid Contract

The Requisite Intent- An assignment takes place when the assignor manifests his intention to make a present transfer of the contractual right. A manifestation of an intent to transfer a right in the future is not an assignment.

No Requirement of Consideration- An assignment, unlike a contract, does not require consideration. If no consideration is given, the assignment may be subject to revocation by the assignor.

Formalities of the Transfer- In the absence of an applicable statute, an assignment need not be evidenced by a writing.

Assignments are excluded from the provisions of UCC Section 2-201 (Statute of Frauds- related to sales of goods). Governed by Section 1-206- under this section, a writing signed by the assignor would be required for the transfer of a **chose in action** of an amount exceeding $5,000.00.

CONTRACTS LAW LECTURE NOTES

Legal Effect of a Valid Assignment

Where a present transfer of an assignable right has been made, the assignor is completely divested of his ownership of the right, and ttile thereto vests in the assignee. The assignee has the same remedies to enforce the right as would have been available to his assignor.

Are there problems relating to the Obligor's Breach? What legal excuses can be raised for the obligor's nonperformance?

In general, an obligor may assert against the assignee all defenses which would have been available against the assignor if there had been no assignment.

Assignee's rights depend on the existence of a valid enforceable contract between the original parties.

Legal Excuses for obligor's nonperformance of his obligation under a valid contract:

- **Failure of conditions**

- **Termination by operation of law**

- **Termination or Modification by the parties**

    o **Restatement 2d Section 338: if the original contract between the parties is still executory, the assignor and obligor** retain the power to make food faith modifications in accordance with reasonable commercial standards even after notification of the assignment is given to the obligor.

- **Obligor's right to claim setoffs-**

  - **Setoff against Assignor-** obligor may assert it against the assignee if it was acquired by him before he received notice of the assignment.

  - **Setoff Against Assignee** (arising out of some other transaction)- he may assert his claim against assignee in addition to any defenses which would have been available against the assignor.

Effect of Article 9 of the UCC-

Sub-assignments- a sub-assignment is a term used to describe a transfer by one who is himself an assignee of the right.

Rights of a Sub-assignee- a sub-assignee steps into the shoes of the original assignor. He has the same remedies to enforce the right as would have been available to the original assignor, and he is subject to the same defenses as might have been asserted against the original assignor.

CONTRACTS LAW LECTURE NOTES

Setoffs against the Subassignee- An obligor may assert against the sub-assignee any setoffs which he had against the original assignor, arising prior to the notice of the sub-assignment. In addition, he may assert setoffs which he has against the sub-assignee himself.

Setoffs against an immediate assignee will NOT be available against a sub-assignee who has given value for the assignment and has no notice of the obligor's claim.

Are there any special problems concerning evocation of a gratuitous assignment, the rights of successive assignees, or warrantees of the assignor?

Revocation of Gratuitous Assignments

An assignment for which no consideration is given may be revoked by the assignor unless certain circumstances exist which operate to make the gratuitous assignment irrevocable.

A gratuitous assignment cannot be revoked if:

- The assignment is in writing and has been delivered to the assigned.

- The assigned right is evidenced by a tangible token which is deemed to represent the right and the token has been delivered to the assignee

- The assignor should reasonably expect the assignment to induce substantial detrimental reliance by the assignee, and the assignee does so rely prior the attempted revocation.

Page | 89

- The assignee, prior to the attempted revocation, has obtained performance from the obligor, or a judgment against the obligor, or a new agreement whereby the obligor has agreed to perform to the assignee.

How is gratuitous assignment revoked?

- Death of assignor

- Subsequent assignment by the assignor of the same right, with or without consideration, or

- Notification of revocation from the assignor received by the assignee or the obligor.

Special Problem

- **Where the assignor assigns the same right to another?**

    o **Where the first assignment is revocable-** it would be revoked by the subsequent assignment and the second assignee would prevaile

- o **Where both assignments are given for a consideration-**

    - ▪ **Majority view-** the assignee who is first in time prevails unless the second assignee, without notice of the other's claim, has obtained one of the following:

        - **Performance from the obligor,**

        - **Judgment against the obligor,**

        - **A new contract with the obligor, or**

        - **Delivery from the assignor of a tangible token representing the right**

    - ▪ **Minority view-** the assignee who first gives notice to the obligor will prevail, provided that he did not know of the prior assignee's claim at the time that the notice was given.

CONTRACTS LAW LECTURE NOTES

- o **Where both assignments are irrevocable gratuitous assignments**- the same rules are applied as in the case where both have been given for a consideration. The conflicting rulings (majority v. minority views) above would be applicable.

- o **Where one assignment is for a consideration and the other is an irrevocable gratuitous assignment**, the one for a consideration will prevail.

Effect of Article 9 of the UCC

Special problem- Warranties of the Assignor

An assignor in an assignment for value impliedly warrants

- That he will do nothing to defeat or impair the value of the assignment,

- That the assigned right actually exists and is subject to no defenses other than those stated or apparent, and

- That any token delivered to the assignee is genuine and what is purports to be. The assignor does not implied warrant that the obligor is solvent or that the obligor will perform.

CONTRACTS LAW LECTURE NOTES

Delegation and Assumption of Duties

Issues related to delegation and assumption of duties:

- **Liability of the Obligee-** Must the oblige accept performance from a person with whom he has not contracted?

    - Is the duty of performance a delegable one?

    - Has it been delegated?

- **Liability of the Delegate-** can the delegate be sued in the event that he refuses to perform?

    - Has the delegate expressly or impliedly assumed the duty of performance?

    - Is the assumption supported by consideration?

- **Legal position of the delegator-** what are the rights and duties of the assignor/delegator following the assignment and delegation?

Must the obligee accept performance from a person whom he has not contracted?

Is the duty of performance a delegable one?

In general, a duty imposed upon an original contracting party may be delegated to a third person <u>unless</u> (1) it is too personal, or (2) delegation is prohibited by the contract, or (3) delegation is prohibited by law.

<u>Personal vs. Impersonal Duties-</u>

A duty is deemed to be too personal for delegation if performance by a third person would <u>materially vary from performance</u> by the original contracting party. (a factual question).

A duty which would ordinarily be too personal for delegation may be validly delegated where the oblige, before or after the delegation, expressly or impliedly assents thereto. Failure to object, with knowledge that the duty is being performed by a third person, may operate as an assent.

If the duties are of an impersonal nature, they may be validly delegated unless the delegation is prohibited by the contract itself or by statute.

<u>Examples-</u>

- <u>Duty to pay cash-</u> impersonal

- <u>Duty in credit transactions-</u> where the personal credit of one party is relied upon by the other- too personal and cannot be delegated.

- <u>Duty to render services-</u> depends on nature of services to be rendered.

CONTRACTS LAW LECTURE NOTES

Personal services- cannot be delegated

Non-personal services- can be delegated

- <u>Duty to Sell Goods</u>- Standard goods- generally can be delegated.

- <u>UCC Section 2-210</u>

The other party may treat any assignment which delegates performance as creating reasonable grounds for insecurity and may without prejudice to his rights against the assignor demand assurances from the assignee

Contractual and Statutory Prohibitions

Has the duty been validly delegated?

- How is the delegation made? A delegation takes place the delegator manifests his intention to presently authority the delegate to perform on his behalf.

- In the absence of a manifested contrary intent, an assignment of a contract carries with it a delegation of duties as well as an assignment of rights.

- Restatement 2d Section 328 provides that an assignment of "all my rights under the contract" or similar general terms carries an implication that delegation of duties is also intended.

- No requirement of consideration or particular formalities.

Can the delegate be sued if he refuses to perform?

In general, a delegation of duties does <u>not</u> in itself impose upon the delegate the obligation to perform. The obligation arises out of the delegate's assumption of the delegator's duties.

<u>An assumption of duty takes place</u> when the delegate, for a consideration, promises the delegator that he will perform on the latter's behalf. The consideration in this promise, in the usual case, will be the assignment of rights under the contract.

Has the delegate expressly or impliedly assumed the duty of performance?

<u>Express or implied assumption of duties</u>- an assumption of duties may be express or implied.

<u>Implied assumption</u>- whether an intent to assume may be inferred from the nature of the transaction.

- <u>Restatement view- Restatement 2d Section 328</u> provides that in the absence of a manifested contrary intent, the mere fact that the assignee/delegate has accepted the assignment will operate as a promise on his part to perform the assignor's duties.

- <u>Contrary view</u>- an intent to assume the duties will not be presumed from the mere fact that there has been the acceptance of an assignment coupled with a delegation. Whether such an assumption is intended by the parties is a factual question.

- <u>UCC position</u>- as to contracts for sale of goods- Section 2-210 is the same as the Restatement rule. The acceptance by the assignee/delegate of an assignment coupled with a delegation constitutes a promise by him to perform the duties delegated.

<u>Is the Assumption Supported by Consideration?</u>

<u>Consideration</u>- the assignment of rights- the delegate's promise to assume the delegator's duties under the contract must be supported by consideration.

In the event the assignment is invalid for any reason, and no other consideration has been given, the delegate is not bound by his promise to assume.

CONTRACTS LAW LECTURE NOTES

Legal Effect of a Valid Assumption

Where there has been an assumption of duties by the delegate and he thereafter fails or refuses to perform, the party to whom performance is due may bring suit as an <u>intended beneficiary</u> of the assumption contract.

Rights and duties of the assignor/delegator following the assignment and delegation?